CW00502676

2012

Everything you need to know
about the Apocalypse

2012

Everything you need to know
about the Apocalypse

MANDA SCOTT

BANTAM PRESS

LONDON · TORONTO · SYDNEY · AUCKLAND · JOHANNESBURG

TRANSWORLD PUBLISHERS
61–63 Uxbridge Road, London W5 5SA
A Random House Group Company
www.transworldbooks.co.uk

First published in Great Britain
in 2011 by Bantam Press
an imprint of Transworld Publishers

Copyright © Manda Scott 2011

Manda Scott has asserted her right under the Copyright,
Designs and Patents Act 1988 to be identified as the author of this work.

A CIP catalogue record for this book
is available from the British Library.

ISBN 9780593069936

Addresses for Random House Group Ltd companies outside the UK
can be found at: www.randomhouse.co.uk
The Random House Group Ltd Reg. No. 954009

The Random House Group Limited supports the Forest Stewardship Council (FSC®), the
leading international forest-certification organization. Our books carrying the FSC label are
printed on FSC®-certified paper. FSC is the only forest-certification scheme endorsed by
the leading environmental organizations, including Greenpeace. Our paper procurement
policy can be found at www.randomhouse.co.uk/environment.

Typeset in Caslon Antique

Printed and bound in Germany by GGP Media GmbH, Pössneck

2 4 6 8 10 9 7 5 3 1

For all those who believe . . .

The first thing you need to know about 2012 is that it's *just* like any other year.

And the second thing you
need to know . . . is that
it really isn't . . .

The year 2012 has been associated with strange apocalyptic prophecies ever since we discovered that the ancient Maya made it the 'end date' of our current 'world age' in their extraordinary Long Count calendar.

('End date' is overstating it somewhat. Better to say that 2012 is when the world is due to roll over into a new cycle – whatever that may mean.)

9

UNITE[D]

MEXICO

Pacific Ocean

North
America

South
America

N

WHERE THE MAYA LIVED

STATES OF AMERICA

Atlantic Ocean

Gulf of Mexico

The Mayan Area

CUBA

Caribbean Sea

BELIZE

GUATEMALA   HONDURAS

NICARAGUA

COSTA RICA

| 0 | MILES | 500 |
| 0 | KILOMETRES | 800 |

The Maya were ferociously clever mathematicians and astronomers who lived in an area extending over what we now call southern Mexico, Guatemala, northern Belize and Honduras.

1 Chichén Itzá
2 Tulum
3 Uxmal
4 Kohunlion

Gulf of Mexico

5 Tikal
6 Yaxchilán
7 Copan

Pacific Ocean

MAYAN ARCHAEOLOGICAL SITES

The Mayan civilization arose in the Yucatán around 2600 BC and reached its zenith around AD 900, after which it collapsed, although parts of it continued to flourish until 1519 . . .

... when Hernán Cortés
arrived with a force of

* 11 ships
* 508 soldiers
* 100 sailors
* 16 horses

And destroyed it all
(mostly).

Then, in 1562, a Franciscan bishop named Diego de Landa ordered and supervised the burning of thousands of irreplaceable Mayan texts.

18

Little remained...

Except three codices and one part codex (the part codex might be a fake), which have survived to the present day.

The codices are made of white limed bark paper and are folded into a concertina shape. Mayan script is painted on with mineral and organic pigments.

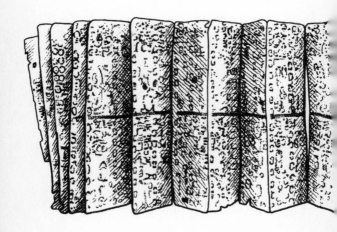

The three intact codices are:

• the **Dresden Codex** (pictured), which is kept in Dresden;

• the **Paris Codex**, which is kept in Paris;

• the **Madrid Codex**, which is kept in . . .

You guessed. Well done.

The Dresden
Codex contains
* almanacs;
* eclipse tables;
* a Venus table
that records when
Venus rises as the
Morning Star;
* a Mars table
(pictured) that records
when the war-planet
appears to go into
retrograde motion.

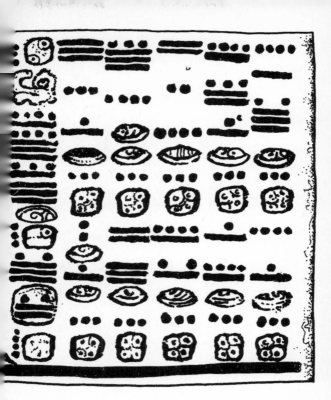

23

From these codices, and from glyphs carved on monuments left behind, we find that the Maya had a highly developed written language, heart-stoppingly beautiful art ...

breathtaking, colossal architecture, a mind-bendingly complicated calendar ... and their mathematics and astronomy rivalled just about anything we can do today.

Temple at Chichén Itzá

While we in the West were still trying to get our heads round the shift from the Julian to the Gregorian calendar, the Maya had calculated the exact length of a solar year to be 365.2422 days.

(Today we estimate it at 365.242198 days.)

They calculated the length of the lunar month at between 29.5302 and 29.5308 days. (Today we have it at 29.53059.)

The Maya counted in base 13 and 20 – because they counted on their toes as well as their fingers – and they used the concept of **zero**, which may seem ordinary

The Mayan counting system

0				
👁				

1	2	3	4	5
•	••	•••	••••	▬

11	12	13	14	15
• ≡	•• ≡	••• ≡	•••• ≡	≡

to you but is a serious step
towards solving the questions of

Life, the Universe
and Everything.

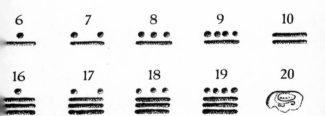

6
7
8
9
10

16
17
18
19
20

The Maya used two calendars: the Short Count and the Long Count. The Short Count, used in daily life, was made up of the ritual 'Tzolk'in' calendar, in which 20 day names and 13 day numbers combined to form a 'short year' of 260 days (which amongst other things is the duration of a human pregnancy from the first missed period to birth).

Interlocking with the 'Tzolk'in' calendar is the 365-day **'Haab' calendar,** which has a vague solar year of 18 months, each of 20 days, plus 5 ceremonial days in which evil deities could wreak havoc on the unwary.

Pop Uo Zip Zotz Zec

Xul Yaxkin Mol Chen Yax

Zac Ceh Mac Kankin Muan

Pax Kayab Kumku Uayeb

The months of the Mayan Haab calendar

Together the Tzolk'in and Haab – which are still in use today – formed a 'calendar round' of 18,980 days, which is roughly 52 years.

Longer dates that involved transits of planets and long periods of time were measured by the **Long Count calendar.**

Units of time in the Mayan calendar

Baktun

Katun

Tun

Uinal

K'in

Ahau

Kankin

36

In the Mayan Long Count

1 day = 1 k'in

20 k'in = 1 uinal (20 days)

18 uinal = 1 tun (360 days)

20 tun = 1 katun (7,200 days)

20 katun = 1 baktun (144,000 days)

13 baktun = 260 katun

(ie 13 x 20 katun – *Are you seeing a pattern here?*)

= 1 calendar round, or 'World Age'.

One World Age = 1,872,000 days or 5,125.36 years

The Mayan Long Count
calendar started on
13th August 3114 BC.

Which was a long, long
time before the beginning
of the Mayan culture.

But by setting their zero date
way back then, it means that
the calendar can roll over to
zero again on the now famous
date . . .

21st December, 2012,
or in Mayan terms
13.0.0.0.0 4 Ahau
3 Kankin

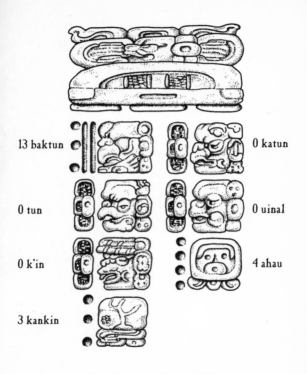

13 baktun

0 katun

0 tun

0 uinal

0 k'in

4 ahau

3 kankin

21st December 2012

And whether you think that's
the end of the world or not ...

there's no doubt that to the ancient Maya it represented the start of a new 13 baktun cycle (or World Age).

But how did the Maya come up with that date in the first place? What made it so special that it was worth setting their zero date 0.0.0.0.0 nearly two millennia before they ever walked the earth?

(Assuming they didn't have crystal balls and didn't know about global warming or currency defaults or Sarah Palin or peak oil?)

We know that the ancient Mayan astronomers studied the Milky Way and gave the name 'Xibalba be' or 'Black Road' to the part we call the 'Dark Rift' (an apparent gap caused by interstellar dust and gas clouds).

And they seem to have been able to predict accurately the precession of the equinoxes. This is the phenomenon by which the rising sun at the spring equinox appears to move backwards through the band of the night sky we call our zodiac (and is probably caused by a very slow wobble in the earth as it spins).

Although it changes with time, the current rate of precession is roughly 50.27 seconds of an arc per year, or 1 degree every 71.6 years.

At the current rate, a complete cycle takes about 25,772 years. The Maya measured it as 5 World Ages of 1,872,000 days per Age.

The Maya knew that in the 36 years on either side of 21st December 2012 the precession of the equinoxes would mean that the rising sun on the winter solstice would appear in conjunction with the mouth of the **Dark Rift** or **Xibalba be.**

50

This is called the
Galactic Alignment.

Which means that the ancient
Maya deliberately backdated
the start of their calendar to
reach the now-famous date at a
point when there's a planetary/
solar/stellar alignment that
occurs for a single 36-year
period every 25,772 years.

Which is
pretty cool,
however you look at it.

The Maya are not alone. Other people who believe that 2012 is a significant date include:

• **ayahuasca dreamers** who have charted the I Ching and say it predicts cycles that end in 2012;

• a selection of tribal shamans, mathematicians, trackers of solar flares and people who have had near-death experiences.

In fact ... since we all lived through the Y2K crisis, 2012 has become the next big

Doomsday Date.

(This doesn't mean that it isn't true, of course ... just that we have heard it all before.)

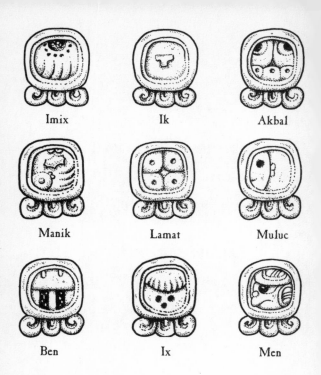

Imix   Ik   Akbal

Manik   Lamat   Muluc

Ben   Ix   Men

Mayan day names

Kan

Chicchan

Cimi

Oc

Chuen

Eb

Cib

Caban

Edznab

Cauac

Ahau

So what do the modern myths
say will happen on this date?

And where do they come
from?

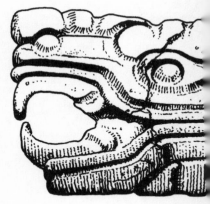

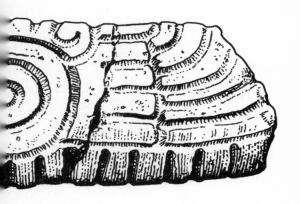

61

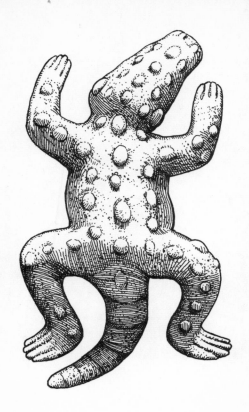

MYTH 1

•

THE END OF A (MAYAN) AGE

According to the Mayan **Popol Vuh** creation story,

the Mayan gods had three
previous attempts at creating
humanity – each of which
failed.

This latest effort began on
13th August, 3114 BC,
at the end of the last 13 baktun
cycle. And if it goes the same
way as the previous three
(which ended in fire, earthquake
and flood respectively) . . .

we're
doomed.

There are people who think that the end of the 13 baktun cycle would herald nothing more for the ancient Maya than a Great Big Party. With any luck they're right.

But . . .

Why would you set the zero date **SO** far back if it wasn't to make the date 13.0.0.0.0 roll over at a time when the rising solstice sun is being devoured by the **galactic serpent?**

None of the sceptics has an
answer to that, although most
of the saner interpreters point
out that it was never going
to be the End of the World,
just the end of an Age – and
nobody is really clear what
that implies.

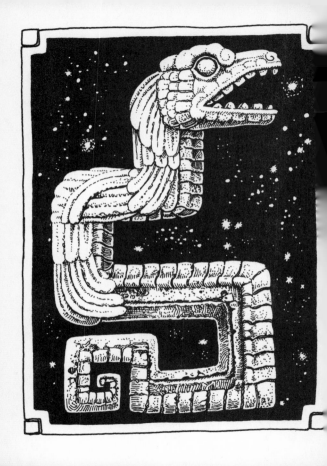

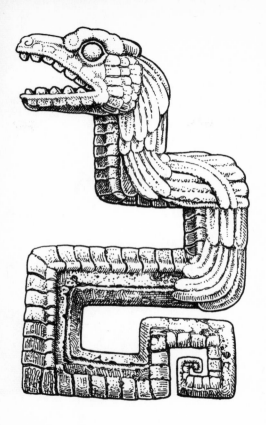

Amongst the doomsayers
there are a fair few who like
the idea that they can take
out huge mortgages . . .

while simultaneously not
paying into a pension in the
hope that the 2012 apocalypse
will erase all their debts
(as well as vaporizing them
in a cloud of solar flares.
Or something).

The rest of us may think that any financial meltdown happened in 2008 . . .

and hope that it won't happen
again. (Though history suggests
we will be sorely disappointed.)

But whatever we may think,
for the true believers 2012 is

EITHER
a time of **transformation**

OR
a time of **cataclysm**

...OR a little bit of both.

MYTH 2

••

THE POLE
SHIFT

'Pole-shift' aficionados
believe that in 2012 there will
be a total geomagnetic
reversal.

During this reversal the earth's mantle will slip around its core of molten iron, causing east to become west and vice versa, and which will in turn reverse the earth's direction of rotation.

The resultant havoc will include massive tsunamis and widespread devastation.

MYTH 3

● ● ●

PLANET X
AND THE
SOLAR
FLARE

Myth 3 is linked to Myth 2 in that some people think the polar shift will be caused not by the galactic alignment . . .

but by the arrival in our solar
system of the planet known
to the Sumerians as Nibiru
and nowadays called *Planet X.*

The theory is that Planet X's orbit causes it to enter our solar system once every 3,600 years and that its presence will disrupt the orbits of the other major planets, thus causing a massive solar flare.

This will cause Jupiter's gases to ignite (fireworks in the sky – yay!), which will turn it into a **Second Sun** – thus fulfilling various second-sun prophecies.

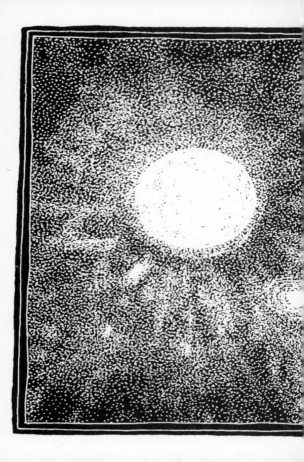

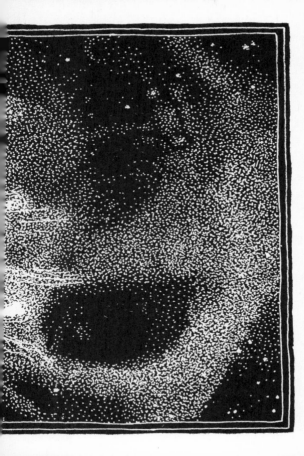

The combined effects of two suns plus an increase in our sun's own cycles of sunspot activity will cause all the **GPS** systems to crash and burn us to a crisp.

94

You may think your car's sat-nav is a heap of rancid slug slime now, but this meltdown will make it seem like a sleek and shiny font of excellence by comparison.

95

According to the True Believers (and there are always some), the promised devastation will be 'More destructive than a nuclear war in which the entire global arsenal of nuclear weapons has been deployed in one blow.'

If it turns out to be true,
there's probably not a lot you
can do, so you may as well
enjoy life while you can.

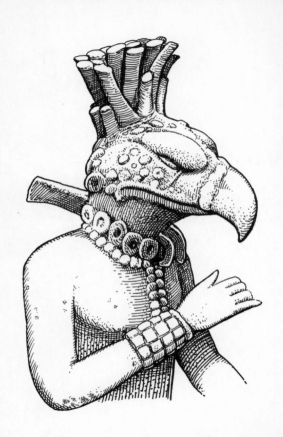

MYTH 4

●●●●

THE FINGER
OF FATE

Casting the chart for That Date, astrologers have found a Saturn/Uranus/Pluto T-square that's distressingly similar to the one that heralded the Great Depression of the 1930s.

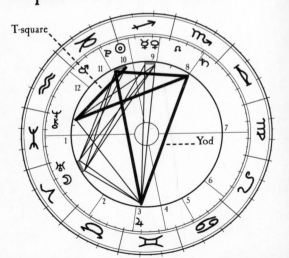

There's also a Finger of Fate (aka a Yod), a narrow kite-like aspect with Sun conjunct Pluto in Capricorn sextile (60°) to Jupiter in Gemini and both quincunx (150°) to Saturn in Scorpio on the opposite side of the chart.

The upshot of all this is that there's a combination of 'powerful but shady forces' (think the Bilderburg Group) trying to control our dwindling resources, and an opposing group of radical thinkers, scientists and internet iconoclasts (think the 'Occupy' movement),

who are becoming more
coherent. If they can condense
their thinking and not get
lost in the hot air of Jupiter,
they could shift us from
our materialism to a more
sustainable future.

We hope.

MYTH 5

TECHNO-
LOGICAL
SINGULARITY

The 'singularity' is when a hyperbolic curve goes vertical.

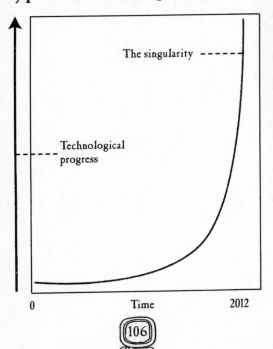

The singularity ------

Technological
progress

0   Time   2012

106

And the 'technological singularity' is when the rate of change of technology goes so fast that we can't keep up. At that point there will be more technological advancement than in all the history of mankind added together.

Or, to put it more simply: some time quite soon we're going to invent a computer that can invent its own successor and build it.

At this point we will be, at best, redundant (because, if nothing else, any super-bright entity that takes one look at the earth is going to decide quite quickly that the single species currently making a hash of just about everything is ... us).

MYTH 6

THE
CRYSTAL
SKULL

Myths of unknown origin
(Aztec, Mayan, Indian – take
your pick) say that thirteen
crystal skulls exist which are
between 5,000 and 35,000
years old and that, when
brought together, they
will either save us – or not
(depending on the myth).

So far only a few skulls of
suitable size and complexity
are known. But the greatest,
the Mitchell-Hedges Skull,
was carved from a single piece
of crystal and is said to be able
to refract light through its eye
sockets as well as incubating
dreams of its creators.

Because they are made of quartz, and computers contain silica chips, there are people who say that the skulls are ancient computers.

Which is an interesting logical leap . . .

But that is nothing at all compared to the amazing properties assigned to the skulls, which encode variously:

• the wisdom of the ancients;

• the prophecies that will enable us to transcend/halt/step through the coming cataclysm;

• the teachings of life and death (which are sorely missing from modern life – as if death was not the only real common denominator).

115

MYTH 7

THE NEXT
EVOLUTIONARY
STEP

It's not just the Maya who say 2012 is a key date. Other people have reached the same conclusion by using:

- the **I Ching** (via the Amazonian hallucinogen ayahuasca)
- the **Bible**
- the **Torah**
- the **Qu'ran**
- near-death experiences, Nostradamus, harmonic convergence studies, crop circles, dreams ...

And the thing they all have
in common is a belief that
the time leading up to 2012 is
the end of an old era and that
the new one will be a period
of spiritual transformation
leading us to the next
evolutionary step.

This theory states that we have reached the end of a very flat evolutionary curve and that the next paradigm shift will be a spiritual one in which we will become psychic/selfless/capable of one-pointed thought. At the dawn of this **Golden Age**, our newly evolved selves will abandon the

ghastly materialism
that is ruining our health, the
planetary ecosystems and our
children's chance of clean
water in order to keep the
bankers in big bonuses.
Which sounds rather wonderful
– and means your yoga classes
were a Very Good Idea.

CONCLUSION

The one thing we can be absolutely sure of is that if we all wake up on 22nd December 2012 and life is exactly the same as it was the day before . . .

22·12·2012

someone will find a link
to a new date in some old
manuscript and the whole
thing will

start all over again.

I propose
2nd February 2022,
or
2.2.22

because I like the number 2 and it reads the same on both sides of the Atlantic.

You can pick your own date.

Enjoy!

ACKNOWLEDGEMENTS

ILLUSTRATIONS:

Patrick Mulrey

pp. 1, 10–11, 13, 18, 20, 22, 26, 30, 34,
36, 39, 41, 58–9, 60, 64, 82, 100, 106

Tomislav Tomic

pp. 2, 16, 52, 62, 72, 80,
86, 92, 98, 104, 110, 116, 122

Thanks to the pioneers of the field, particularly
John Major Jenkins and Geoff Stray.

Astrological insight came from
Tracy Thursfield.

With thanks to Phil Lord for the design, without
which this would be half the book it is . . .

For further reading, start at:
http://www.diagnosis2012.co.uk